The Illuminati

The Ultimate Illuminati Guide With All You Need to Know About the Illuminati and Its Best Conspiracies!

Table Of Contents

Introduction

I want to thank you and congratulate you for downloading the book, *"The Illuminati: The Ultimate Guide with All You Need to Know About the Illuminati and Its Best Conspiracies!"*

This book contains helpful information about the Illuminati and its history, goals, and beliefs as well as some famous conspiracy theories associated with the order.

Many times, the Order of the Illuminati and other secret societies have been the center of debates specifically on their influence in human history. The number of people questioning whether the Illuminati rules the world in secret or that it's just a myth has grown. The facts about the Illuminati have been turned into misinformation and misconceptions, which has resulted in difficulty carrying out objective research about the Order.

In general, the term "Illuminati" is used to depict an elite group, which is said to be ruling the world. Although some people know the meaning behind the term, many individuals, organizations, and sects are confused about the Order's relation with the Freemasonry, its goals, practices, beliefs, and secrecy.

The search for the truth about the Order of the Illuminati almost always ends up as a grueling task. This is because most resources that offer information about the Order either deny or ridicule anything associated with the Illuminati. Some resources even substantiate information or data that are only based on misconceptions and rumors. At any rate, many researchers end up with a misrepresentation of the truth about the Order of the Illuminati.

Thus, it can be a great challenge to obtain an unbiased truth about the Order of the Illuminati, given that its history is mostly rewritten and even modified by people in power. In addition, just like any other secret society, the Order of the Illuminati is supposed to be a secret.

This book attempts to establish a more factual picture of the Order of the Illuminati based on credible information, which is mostly written and accounted for by some initiates of Secret Societies.

Thanks again for downloading this book. I hope you enjoy it!

Chapter 1:
The Illuminati Origins

The term, Illuminati is the plural form of the Latin word, *illuminatus*, which means "enlightened." Throughout history, the term has been referred to as a secret society called the Bavarian Illuminati, which was established on May 1, 1776. The goals of the society were to dispute the religious influence as well as superstition and deception over abuses of state power and public life.

During the late 1700s, the Illuminati, Freemasonry, and other secret societies were interdicted through the Edict of Charles Theodore, the Bavarian ruler with support from the Roman Catholic Church. Several years after the interdiction, many conservative and religious groups claimed that the Illuminati still existed and continued in concealment or under cover. These groups also spread the information that the Illuminati were the instigators of the French Revolution.

Subsequently, the term Illuminati now pertains to different organizations that are claiming to have connections to the original Bavarian Illuminati or other secret societies. On the other hand, the so-called connections of these organizations to the Bavarian Illuminati are not supported by any kind of evidence.

The Illuminati are said to conspire in ruling and controlling the affairs of the world through orchestrating events and utilizing agents in corporations and governments. The purpose of this is to acquire political influence and power as well as to constitute a New World Order.

The History

On February 6, 1748, Adam Weishaupt was born in Ingolstadt, Bavaria. He was seven years old when his father died. Weishaupt was then entrusted to his godfather, Baron Ickstatt, who provided him with his early education in the hands of the Jesuits. At the time, the Society of Jesus, which was directed by the Jesuits was considered the most powerful group known for its revolutionary methods and inclinations to conspiracy. The Society of Jesus also dominated the educational system and political arena of Bavaria.

The beliefs of the Society of Jesus resembled those of the secret brotherhoods, which it opposed. For instance, it acted with initiation rites, degrees, esoteric symbols, and elaborate rituals. In addition, a number of countries suppressed the Society of Jesus due to its revolutionary inclinations.

In 1773, Ickstatt employed his authority and great influence to place Weishaupt as the chairperson of canon law at the University of Ingolstadt. During that time, the Jesuits greatly dominated the institution. The position that Weishaupt assumed was traditionally held by influential Jesuits.

Weishaupt learned to embrace the philosophies of the Age of Enlightenment, which caused him to be in disagreement with the Jesuits, resulting in various types of political drama. On the other hand, in spite of his conflict with the Jesuits, he learned many things about the organization and their revolutionary methods for gaining power. Due to the influence of the Jesuits, specifically their subversive methods, it crossed Weishaupt's mind to establish a Secret Society.

There are opposing views as to the relationship of Weishaupt with the Jesuits. Some authors say that he sought to bring down the powerful hold of the Jesuits on Bavaria. He believed that overthrowing all government institutions and religious organizations across the globe could be beneficial to everyone through replacing them with a global committee of "initiates." Thus, in order to achieve his objectives, he would utilize the methods of the Jesuits against them. Others, however, claim that it was the Jesuits who used Weishaupt to preserve their dominance in Bavaria.

Weishaupt also became well-versed in occult mysteries and Hermitism as he continued his studies. The power of the mysterious knowledge appealed to him greatly; thus, he believed that in order to spread his views, he would use the Masonic lodges as his venue. Although Weishaupt attempted to become a Freemason, the idea did not linger in his mind for long.

On May 1, 1776, Weishaupt founded the Order of the Illuminati, also known as the Bavarian Illuminati, with the goal of overthrowing all political institutions and religious organizations in the world, replacing them with a group of his initiates. The intention of Weishaupt's organization was to discard riches, hierarchy, and rank to quickly achieve universal happiness. According to Weishaupt, the goal of the Illuminati was to make the human race as one family. The world would be home to reasonable men, and rulers and nations would be no more, all without the need for violence.

The Bavarian Illuminati

Weishaupt began the Order of the Illuminati with just five members. However, the Order became known across the globe as a leading political organization just a few years after it was founded. It gained many powerful connections as powerful noblemen, rich industrials, influential deciders, and mysterious occultists banded themselves in the Order and took part in its conspiratorial goals. According to some historians, the Order became very successful in just a few years due to Weishaupt's affiliation with Cagliostro, an occultist deemed to be the most powerful one at the time, whom Weishaupt had a secret meeting with.

Originally, the Order of the Illuminati or the Bavarian Illuminati was composed of three principal grades or degrees. These were the Novice, Minerval, and Illuminated Minerval. Every grade or degree functioned differently based on specific objectives; however, all grades or degrees were designed to assure total dominance and control to the pyramid's highest point or apex.

The Illuminati began their expansion with this basic structure. Weishaupt made sure that everything was in place in order to achieve the significant objective of infiltrating the Freemasonry.

Chapter 2:
The Three Grades Of The Order

The following is a brief description of the three grades of the Order of the Illuminati:

Novice Bavarian

Illuminati members at the entry level are said to be drawn and introduced to the Order through the utilization of appealing words about the quest for betterment and wisdom and occult lore. Novice Illuminati members were also introduced to a hierarchy, which is consistently monitored as well as controlling, just like the system that Jesuits used. In this grade, the political goals of the Order are not mentioned.

According to scholars and historians, once a novice is enrolled, the instruction is to be in the enroller's hands. The enroller keeps the identity of the rest of the superiors well-hidden from the novice. During the novitiate period, the aim of the Order is to improve and perfect the moral character of the novice, induce his interest in commendable factors that thwart the acts and systems of evil men, expand his human and social principles, and help worthy men in finding suitable places in the world.

Furthermore, during the novitiate period, the need of maintaining absolute secrecy and respecting the Order's affairs is instilled in the novice. After which, the novice will then be submitted to subdue his egotistic interests and views while being under consummate obedience and respect to his superiors.

One of the most significant parts of a novice's responsibility is a detailed report about himself. This is for the Order's archives. The report should include the novice's complete information about his family and personal career. It should also include remote items such as the names of the novice's personal enemies, and the occurrence of the enmity, titles of books he owns, his strong and weak character points, the names of his parents, siblings, and relatives, and the dominant passions of his parents among others. The novice is also required to do monthly reports that cover the benefits he had received from the Order as well as the services he rendered.

In order to advance to the higher grades, the novice should remain as a novitiate for about two years and render his service in the recruitment work. His advancement will be based on his performance and success in his recruiting efforts. When the novice is able to recruit and enroll another novice, he will be the latter's superior. Once the superiors have proven that the novice is worthy of advancement, he will then be initiated to the Minerval grade or degree.

Minerval

The term "Minerval" comes from Minerva, who is known as the Roman goddess of poetry, wisdom, weaving, medicine, commerce, magic, crafts, and music. Minerva is often associated with an owl, which is considered her sacred creature. The owl, on the other hand, is known for its wisdom. Minerva is popularly depicted as an ancient symbol of the mysteries in various places such as the Great Seal of California and the Library of Congress.

The Order's second grade or degree involves indoctrination. In this grade, the initiates are taught about the Order's spiritual principles; however, they still do not have sufficient information about the real goals or objectives of Weishaupt and his close administrators.

In the Minerval grade, the initiates are expected to free their minds of any lingering suspicion about the Order's ultimate objective, which is to bring down the rich and powerful or overthrow political institutions and religious organizations. In the ceremony of initiation, the initiate pledges to be serviceable to humanity; to maintain an obedience to all the superiors and the Order's rules; to maintain an absolute silence and fidelity; and to sacrifice all personal interests for the society.

One of the privileges of the minervals is that they are able to meet a few of their superiors who are known as the Illuminated Minervals. The minervals can become involved in discussions with their superiors from which they obtain a great source of motivation.

Illuminated Minerval

There is only a selected few from the Minervals who advance to the grade of Illuminated Minerval. In this grade, the once novice and initiate become superiors and are given tasks that they should specifically accomplish in preparing them to function in the "real world." The bulk of the work of the Illuminated Minerval members is mainly the study of mankind as well as the perfection of methods.

A small group of Minervals is entrusted to each Illuminated Minerval member to be analyzed and guided towards a particular direction. Thus, the Order's lower-grade members are the subjects for methods and techniques, which can be employed generally to the masses.

The grade 'Illuminated Minerval' involves the mastery of the art of leading or directing men. In order to accomplish being the director of men's consciences and become expert psychologists, members should take note of the actions and constantly examine the purposes, virtues, desires, and faults of the group of Minervals assigned to them. The members are provided with a complicated set of instructions as their guidance in their task. Furthermore, the candidates are expected to work on their progressive purification in life as they advance in the Order.

Apart from this, the members of the Illuminated Minerval grade come together by themselves on a monthly basis to discuss reports regarding their assigned groups of Minervals. The records of the Minerval assemblies are also reviewed, amended, and eventually passed on to the Order's superior officers. At this meeting, the members also discuss the methods that can be used to achieve the best outcome in their work and solicit counsel from each other about complicated and embarrassing events.

The Illuminati and the Freemasonry

A year after he founded his Order of the Illuminati, Weishaupt joined the Freemasonry in the lodge of Theodore of Good Counsel in Munich. In this lodge, Weishaupt was able to propagate his views successfully and managed to influence the lodge into the Illuminist order.

In 1790, Weishaupt established an alliance between the Illuminati and Freemasonry as Baron Adolf Franz Friedrich Knigge, a prominent German diplomat and member of the Freemasonry was initiated into the Order. In turn, the Order adapted the Masonic association and efficient organizational skills of Knigge. However, the influence of Knigge upon the Order brought two substantial consequences. He managed to revise the Order's hierarchy by creating new higher grades while maintaining the original ones and allowed the Masonic lodges to be fully integrated into the system.

Knigge incorporated the Freemasonry grades in the second grade of the Illuminati, which made the Freemasonry a part of a more extensive Illuminist structure. The purpose of this was to provide an opportunity for members of various departments of the Masonic family to advance to the higher grades of the Order. Although Knigge did not change the grade Novice of the Order, he added a printed communication, which was given to the new recruits.

Knigge devised a new system, which the Freemasons and other influential figures found appealing. Thus, the Order obtained considerable momentum and became a powerful movement.

On the other hand, Weishaupt was not able to enjoy the success of his Order for long. The Bavarian government set up an edict that outlawed all types of societies, communities, and brotherhoods that functioned without obtaining the authorization of the law. This was in light of suspicions that the Illuminati were conspiring against the government institutions and religious organizations all over Europe.

In addition, there was also an internal dissonance between Weishaupt and the Order's higher superiors that led to discordance and disputes. Some members decided to go against the Illuminati and proceeded to the authorities, testifying against the Order.

In 1788, twelve years after its creation, the Bavarian Illuminati were said to be dissolved through the government's use of aggressive legislation. The Bavarian government also filed criminal charges against the members of the Order. On the other hand, while many believed that the Illuminati were concluded during this time, it should not be forgotten that the Order had its chance to propagate beyond the borders of Bavaria. It should be noted that the Order was able to reach Masonic lodges all over Europe. Thus, the Illuminati were never dissolved or destroyed. It only went underground. In fact, a year after it was thought to be destroyed, the Illuminati proved that it was very much alive and potent through the French Revolution.

The Illuminati and the French Revolution

In 1789, the French Monarchy was overthrown violently, symbolizing the defeat of the traditional institutions and the victory of Jacobinism and Illuminism. Later on, the Declaration of Human Rights acknowledged the Masonic and Illuminist values, accepting them into the core of the French government. Thus, the new motto of the country became "Liberté, Égalité et Fraternité," which translates to Freedom, Equality and Brotherhood. For centuries, this motto was used in French Masonic lodges.

Several occult symbols composed the official document of the Declaration of Human Rights. These symbols were said to refer to Secret Societies. The document contained the All-Seeing Eye within a triangle symbol, surrounded by the light of the blazing star Sirius, which is located above everything else. Below the document's title is an esoteric symbol of a serpent eating its own tail. This symbol is known as an Ouroboros, which is associated with Alchemy, Hermetism, and Gnosticism, the Masonry's core teachings. A red Phrygian cap is found right below the Ouroboros. This is said to represent Illuminist revolutions around the world. Finally, the entire document is protected by Masonic pillars.

Motion Up Against the Illuminati

While many thought the Bavarian Illuminati were destroyed, the ideas of the Order still became evident across Europe. The Illuminati apparently lived through the thriving Freemasons and Rosicrucians. During this time, Europe was experiencing a violent agitation given that the mechanisms of power were being steered by a new class of people. Consequently, many critics came forth and revealed to the masses those who were responsible for the changes occurring in Europe.

One of the first individuals who emerged against the Illuminati was Leopold Hoffman, a Freemason who claimed that his Brotherhood was corrupted by the Illuminati. In his journal, Wiener Zeitschrift, Hoffmann published a series of articles with various claims. In one of his articles, Hoffman claimed that the French Revolution was the result of the Illuminati's propaganda, which the latter plotted for years. He also claimed that although the lower grades of the Illuminati were discarded, its highest degrees were still active. Hoffman added that his brotherhood, the Freemasonry was being subdued and transformed for the benefit of the Illuminati.

Many individuals emerged after Hoffman published its articles. In 1797, a Scottish physician, inventor, mathematician, and Freemason by the name of John Robinson came forth and published his book entitled, "Proofs of a Conspiracy Against all the Religions and Governments of Europe Carried on in the Secret Meetings of the Freemasons, Illuminati, and Reading Societies." Robinson was a devout Freemason who became disillusioned after finding out that the Illuminati infiltrated his brotherhood.

In the same year, a French Jesuit priest, Augustin Barrel, published his book, "Mémoires pour servir à l'histoire du

Jacobisime." Barrel's book focused on the connection of the Bavarian Illuminati to the French Revolution. He also deciphered the slogan "Liberty and Equality," tracing back to the early Templars. Barrel claimed that in the Illuminati's higher degrees, liberty and equality were not only depicted as "war against kings and thrones" but also "war against Christ and His altars." Barrel also gave out information about the Illuminati's takeover of the Freemasonry.

The Illuminati's Propagation Across America

According to most scholars, the Founding Fathers of the United States of America were part of Secret Societies such as Freemasonry, Rosicrucianism, or others. As some of the Founding Fathers traveled to Europe, they became knowledgeable and obtained extensive information about the doctrines of the Illuminati. Two of the most prominent founding fathers who were said to have Illuminist associations were Benjamin Franklin and George Washington.

As the ambassador of the United States to France, Benjamin Franklin went to Paris and stayed there from 1776 to 1785. During these years, the Bavarian Illuminati were very active. Franklin became the Grand Master of the Les Neufs Soeurs lodge, which was associated with the Grand Orient of France. The Masonic organization that Franklin joined was said to be the headquarters of the Bavarian Illuminati in France. It was also said to be highly influential in the organization of French support for both the American and French revolutions.

In 1799, George Washington was warned of the Illuminati's plan to bring down all government institutions and religious organizations. German minister G.W. Snyder received a reply from Washington saying that he was already aware of the doctrines of the Illuminati as well as its nefarious plan.

However, Washington also said in his reply that he believed no lodges in the United States of America were contaminated with the Illuminati's objectives and principles. It was very obvious from Washington's reply that he was aware of the presence of the Illuminati as well as its principles. While he believed that the Masonic institutions in the United States remained unchanged or uncontaminated by the Illuminati's doctrines, Washington confessed that some individuals might have consented and joined the propagation of the Illuminati in America.

The Illuminati Today

In this day and age, the term Illuminati is often referred to as the small group of influential individuals who are geared towards the establishment of a One World Government, which has a single religion and a single currency. However, there is no clear or precise information if this group comes from the original Bavarian Illuminati or if its goals and principles are the same as the Weishaupt's Order. On the other hand, many people believe that whether or not the term Illuminati is used to refer to the occult elite, the important thing to discern is the continuity of the Illuminati.

In the event that the Order of the Illuminati still exists today, the question is now about the form it takes. Most scholars believe that there are some modern Secret Societies that claim to be scions of Illuminism; one of which is the Ordo Templi Orientis (OTO). Some researchers, on the other hand, believe that there are hidden Orders, which form the Illuminati on top of the 33 degrees of Freemasonry in sight. Given that both the Illuminati and the Freemasonry are "secret" societies, it can be hard to obtain specific and accurate details about them.

Accordingly, the political objectives of the modern Illuminati are much more obvious today. Researchers claim that a restricted group is entrusted with creating substantial decisions and policies. These days, there are global organizations and committees that maneuver elected officials. Their primary objective is to establish global economic and social policies where a non-elected shadow government will be the center of world power. This government will be composed of the elites. This is also becoming a trend nowadays.

Based on research about the modern Illuminati, the main councils and groups composed of elites include the following: Chatham House, the World Economic Forum, the Trilateral Commission, the Brookings Institution, and the Bilderberg Group. The Bohemian Club, on the other hand, is known to carry out informal meetings and gatherings with the elites, performing strange rituals and ceremonies. The Club uses an Owl as its insignia. As mentioned earlier, the Bavarian Illuminati also make use of an Owl, which is the Minerval seal.

Many researchers are now noticing that most, if not, all the attendees and members of these exclusive clubs belong to the world's elite. The gatherings compose of the most influential and powerful CEOs, intellectuals, and politicians. Most of them are scions of powerful dynasties that take over the modern economies' significant aspects including the mass media, banking systems, and oil industry.

Based on the book of Fritz Springmeier, "Bloodlines of the Illuminati," the modern Illuminati is created from the scions of thirteen influential families. The ancestors of these families were known to have associations or ties with the original Bavarian Illuminati. The 13 bloodlines mentioned in the book include: the Kennedys, the Rockefellers, the Van Duyns, the Astors, the DuPonts, the Bundys, the Onassis, the Li, the

Collins, the Reynolds, the Freemans, the Russells, and the Rothschilds.

Given the political and material resources owned by these families, there is no uncertainty that some, if not, all of these families possess considerable power in the world. It is highly possible that these families form the core of today's Illuminati.

Chapter 3:
The Illuminati: Purpose and Goals

In this chapter, the purpose of the Illuminati that will be discussed is based on those claiming to be members of the Illuminati who break their silence from time to time. They choose specific persons to convey their ideas and contradict those who judge them. However, these members maintain that they are always in hiding as they have always been to protect themselves from those who want to do them harm.

On the other hand, the goals of the Illuminati that will be tackled in this chapter is based on the book "Conspirators' Hierarchy: The Committee of 300," which is written by Dr. John Coleman, who travelled many countries to unmask the entire secret upper-level parallel government. He claims that this parallel government runs both the United States of America and Britain.

Illuminati Purpose

According to some alleged members of the Illuminati, the primary purpose of the Order is to ensure the current survival of human beings. They believe that even the human species is bound to be extinct; as such, humans strive to protect themselves from extinction. These alleged members claim that although countries have borders, all humans are members of one biological family, which makes them collective. Furthermore, they claim that every individual is important to the survival of the human species just as the great kings and queens were significant to their realms.

However, according to these alleged Illuminati members, human beings are naturally affected by emotion, imbalance, and instinct. For this reason, an individual has the tendency to turn on another person for intentions that may never matter in many years. As such, the purpose of the Illuminati is to protect the interests of the human species as a whole. It runs various programs and departments for the welfare of all people from all generations and in all places. The Illuminati claim to secure the current dominance of human beings over other creatures and predators on Earth.

Illuminati Goals

According to the book of Dr. John Coleman entitled "Conspirators' Hierarchy: The Committee of 300," the Illuminati had established ways and means to create a New World Order based on their beliefs and principles. Coleman also claims that the Illuminati had built their groups of accomplices to carry out their plans. Coleman listed twenty-one goals of the Illuminati based on his research and the opportunities given to him to access unusual documents pertaining the Illuminati.

First, the Illuminati intends to create a One World Government, which is composed of only one church and a single currency under the control of the Order.

Second, the Illuminati intends to destroy completely the identity and pride of each nation. This is because it is only through total destruction of these factors that the people will accept and adapt a "super-national" world government.

Third, the Illuminati intends to destroy all religions, specifically the denominations of Christianity. Therefore, the Order will create just one global religion.

Fourth, the Illuminati intends to create thought-control methods based on a goal of producing human robots who will address external impulses and direction.

Fifth, the Illuminati intends to stop all systems of industrialization except the computer and service sectors. The goal is to create a "post-industrial zero growth society" while other industry branches will focus on third world countries.

Sixth, the Illuminati intends to promote and eventually legalize the use of prohibited drugs as well as create art from pornography that will initially be accepted and finally viewed as completely normal.

Seventh, the Illuminati intends to desolate larger cities similar to the bloodbaths in Cambodia that was allegedly perpetuated by Pol Pot, who was a socialist revolutionary.

Eighth, the Illuminati intends to suppress further scientific developments with the exception of those serving the Order's purposes and objectives.

Ninth, the Illuminati intends to cause premature deaths of three billion people by 2050. This will be carried out either by starvation and sickness in underdeveloped countries or through regional warfare in highly-developed countries. Under the Illuminati's direction, the Committee of 300 authorized the U.S. Secretary of State under Carter's regime, Cyrus Vance to write a paper about population reduction, specifically the manner that it can be done. Vance's paper was entitled "Global 2000 Report," which was acknowledged and approved by President Carter and then Secretary of State, Edwin Muskie. The Global 2000 Report specified conditions, one of which is that the U.S. Population should be cut down by 100 million people in 2050.

Tenth, the Illuminati intends to deaden the morale of people and further discourage the working class through a large scope of unemployment. Thus, the unemployed will be induced to drug usage and addiction to alcohol. Moreover, the youth will be urged to go against the state of affairs, leading to weakened or disintegrated families through drug use and unrestrained music.

Eleventh, the Illuminati intends to force people to deal with one crisis after another in order to stop them from discerning their fate. Thus, the people will learn to depend on the One Government as they become overwhelmed by many unfortunate situations. The Federal Emergency Management Agency (FEMA) is already in existence as an authority for crisis management.

Twelfth, the Illuminati intends to bring in new cults, which will support the existing ones.

Thirteenth, the Illuminati intends to support Protestantism or Christian fundamentalism, which will eventually support the objectives of the Zionist Israeli state.

Fourteenth, the Illuminati intends to promote the propagation of religious organizations such as the Sikhs and the Muslim Brotherhood as well as to implement thought-control experiments. These experiments will be similar to the mass murder/suicide of more than 900 people under the command of James Warren "Jim" Jones, an American cult leader. Jones ordered his people to make a concoction of grape-flavored Flavor Aid and cyanide and drink it. He also ordered his people to inject the same concoction to children of certain age.

Fifteenth, the Illuminati intends to spread religious freedom by promoting a "world in order" so that all other existing religions, specifically Christianity will be doubted and undermined. The "Theology of Liberation" is said to be the beginning of this Order's goal.

Sixteenth, the Illuminati intends to arouse the prostration of the world economy, leading to a total political disorder.

Seventeenth, the Illuminati intend to rule over all domestic and international policies of the United States of America.

Eighteenth, the Illuminati intend to provide the greatest support to supranational institutions such as the United Nations Organization (UNO), the Bank for International Settlements (BIS), the International Monetary Fund (IMF), and the International Court of Justice (ICJ) among others. In addition, the Illuminati plan to systematically destroy or bring local and national institutions under UNO's controlling umbrella.

Nineteenth, the Illuminati intend to bring down and take over all governments with the goal of dividing and destroying internally every nation's sovereignty.

Twentieth, the Illuminati intend to bring about international terrorism as well as negotiate with terrorists each time they carry out their terrorism activities.

Twenty-first, the Illuminati intends to rule over the educational system of the United States of America and eventually destroy it completely.

According to Coleman, the agents of the Illuminati operated and still operate under the disguise of opposing to Zionism and the government.

Chapter 4:
Illuminati Beliefs

The beliefs of the Illuminati are based on four principal tenets. These include the tenet of freedom and belief, the tenet of God and Satan, the tenet of money and abundance, and the tenet of value and trade.

Tenet of Freedom and Belief

Other than the sovereignty of the human species, the Order of the Illuminati has no other belief. According to scholars, the Order of the Illuminati is an elite enterprise of global, influential, and powerful individuals as opposed to the common idea that it is a religion, church, charity organization, or political group. The Illuminati is said to work to protect the interests of the human species alone; thus, it is self-governing and not affiliated with any type of human division such as political and religious variations. Given that its purpose is to protect the interests of the human species, it operates solely for such purpose and does not make demands of anyone with regard to morality, belief, or personal worship.

The Illuminati believes that all those who are loyal to its purpose, objectives, and ideals are free to choose their life paths as long as it is always for the benefit of the human species' interests. Today, members of the Illuminati are referred to as followers of Illuminatism, who give up any geographical, generational, and religious differences, working as a single unit with a number of distinguishable parts.

Tenet of God and Satan

For the Illuminati, faith is an impression upon something, which could not be proven. According to the Order of the

Illuminati, people follow commandments of a particular religious text from a source, which cannot be verified or an author whom they have not met or spoken to. Furthermore, many people believe in a spiritual being because they were spoken to of miracles by someone who was not even alive when such miracles were performed.

On the other hand, the Illuminati claims that to denounce faith is an act of foolishness, for faith is not confined to religion alone. The religious foundation of the Illuminati is based on the difficult problem of faith and doubt. The Order of the Illuminati does not speculate whether or not a god exists; however, the focus of its faith is on the amelioration of the human species on Earth. The decisions made by the Illuminati are based on a study of data as well as evidence, which are factors that can be changed from an all-knowing figure to guide the actions and future of human beings.

The Illuminati denies the deceitful public perception that the Order is affiliated by either God or Satan and that the misconducts committed by many people are under their command. In addition, the Order of the Illuminati neither accepts nor denies any god and does not consider one to be higher than the other. It reiterates that the Order operates solely for the amelioration of the human species.

The Illuminati also denies rumors of being involved in heinous acts such as violent rituals and human sacrifices. The Order claims to be dedicated solely to the preservation of mankind, although their members are free to serve any god they choose. Given that human sacrifices or any act that contradicts the preservation of the human species are prohibited by the Order.

Whether or not a god must exist for its members, the Illuminati simply states that doing what is good for the benefit of mankind is what matters the most. Should a higher power exist, the act of goodness will be rewarded.

Tenet of Money and Abundance

The Order of the Illuminati believes that a person's worldly influence is quantified by money. This elite collective of influencers claim that many people who have never experienced wealth often propagate negative insinuation with regard to money; that is, it is often the "root of all evil." However, the Illuminati oppose to this statement given that money can actually solve the most excruciating events in one's life. For instance, mothers use the money to take care of their children's material needs. Artists are rewarded with money for their hardships and years of practice of their craft. Thus, the Illuminati believe that money is not evil.

On the other hand, the Order claims that the manner in which the money is used determines whether it is good or evil. Given that money has no voice, soul, or feelings, it cannot dictate how it should be used. As such, money is either good or evil, depending on how a person makes use of it. This is to say that as much as money can be utilized to harm a person, it can also be used to heal. In a more precise example, beggars consider money as a source of food and life while dictators consider money as an instrument for weapons and even death.

The Order of the Illuminati believes that every person should pursue abundance based on the idea that the Earth has plenty of riches for everyone to enjoy. The Order compares an abundant life to a glass with water. Life is abundant if like the glass, it is filled to the brim and the water spills over its edges. Therefore, when an individual has an abundant life, he/she has the freedom to help others because he/she no longer needs to help himself/herself.

In terms of the connection between money and abundance, the Illuminati believes that money can be measured by those who bear it. For instance, a hundred is a lot for a beggar; a hundred is little for a millionaire; and hundreds of thousands allow a billionaire save lives through giving basic needs such as food, shelter, and medicine. However, if an individual is poor or has a scarce life, he/she cannot save anyone, not even his/her own life.

Tenet of Value and Trade

The Order of the Illuminati considers things that cost nothing as worthless. However, most costs do not demand for money as payment. For instance, a powerful mind costs a person's hours spent in studying and reading. A healthy body costs a person's effort and time spent in preparing food and doing exercises. On the other hand, the Illuminati also believes that for easier trade, money provides a numeric value to almost everything on Earth; thus, making money a tradable currency of both effort and knowledge.

The Order of the Illuminati believes that the sole purpose of money is to assign a mathematical value on effort and knowledge of the use of trade. For example, a law student pays money to a school in order to obtain the knowledge required for his future career. The lawyer's knowledge obtained from teachers is paid with money. Successively, money can be used to pay for other people's effort and knowledge, even when they do not need a lawyer's service.

Therefore, the belief of the Illuminati with regard to value and trade is that things that have value are never free; otherwise they would be valueless.

Chapter 5:
Illuminati's Symbols

The Order of the Illuminati makes use of symbols, which are viewed by most people as artwork, visual media, and/or architecture. On the other hand, the Illuminati claim that its symbols function as noble instructions for people who choose to follow the Light. This chapter will discuss each symbol in detail to give a clearer understanding of what the symbols mean.

The Pyramid

The Illuminati makes use of the Pyramid as a symbol indicating that each person is a part of the most complex mechanism. Each level of the Pyramid is important; that is, without its foundation, there will be no structure at all. The Pyramid reminds each person that the journey of life begins at the bottom. However, only a few rise above or advance to the next level. Thus, as a person steps up the Pyramid, he/she is made aware of his/her part on Earth.

The Eye

The Illuminati makes use of the Eye as a symbol indicating one that sees and knows all. It is located at the center of the Light. The Order of the Illuminati claims that the Light is fixed on truth and those who follow it becomes the center of the Universal Design of this planet. The Eye, according to the Illuminati, can be compared to a shepherd who sees and knows all his flock.

The Light

The Illuminati makes use of the Light as a symbol indicating an ever-present guidance in a world filled with hardship, war, and confusion. Everyone seeking the glow of the Light reflects it into the dark spaces of the world. In the same way, those who follow it for the amelioration of the human species will be rewarded by the unseen and unnamed higher power.

The Eternal/Circle

The Illuminati makes use of the Eternal or Circle as a symbol indicating its duty to the world, which have gone through centuries and survived the most conventional government bodies. According to the Illuminati, although their efforts are not recognized or acknowledged, it continues to shape major movements on Earth. The Order claims of guiding the human species and protecting it from extinction. The Eternal indicates the continuity of the Illuminati to stand eternally.

Chapter 6:
Illuminati: Good or Evil?

The most common notion about the Order of the Illuminati is that it is responsible for generations of deceptions, violent disturbances, and conspiracies. Even in the most developed countries, many believe that the Illuminati was able to cause chaos within the borders. Today, there are groups of individuals that have one thought about the Illuminati; that is, the Order still exists and operates most, if not, all powerful entities about the across the globe to fulfill their objective of having a One World Government. Judging from what most people say, the Illuminati appear to be evil.

On the other hand, there are also a few people who think twice about the real nature of the Illuminati. Although most of the beliefs and objectives of the Illuminati, if truth be told, are far beyond the norms of this society, some of their goals are quite interesting and workable. As such, there are a small number of people who agree with that the Illuminati is not as bad as many think.

For instance, this small number of people claim that the Illuminati was created to preserve the human species and not its morality or comfort. Those who are willing to join the Order are guided and directed to the Light; however, there are not forced to do so. The Illuminati believes that only the slaves are subjected to obey their masters and that humans do not deserve slavery.

People who indicate their belief in the Illuminati claim that the elite order is not elected by those it represents. This is because the Order's authority does not call for approval from anybody. Illuminati members, just like any other human being or group of individuals are residents of the Earth; however, the Order stands up and fights for the benefit of mankind given that no one else is willing to do the task. In addition, the primary concern of the Illuminati is the result of their efforts to protect the human species from extinction.

Whether the Order of the Illuminati is good or evil depends on one's own point of view. There may be some who find that the Illuminati's goals, objectives, and practices too radical, violent, and aggressive while others seem to agree with the feasibility of the Order's plans for humanity and the world. It all depends on one's own belief with respect to how the world can be a better place to live in.

Chapter 7:
The Illuminati Conspiracy Theory

Synopsis

Today, many people are showing great interest in the Illuminati and disseminating both positive and negative information about the Order, specifically on the Internet. Most of the information emerging today is about the involvement of the Illuminati in global industries, politics, entertainment, and media.

Even before the advancement in technology, authors and conspiracy theorists believed that the Order of the Illuminati still existed and in secret just like how it started. Some of the authors and conspiracy theorists include Augustin Barruel, David Icke, William Guy Carr, Mark Dice and Nesta Helen Webster. Incidentally, the theory of Webster claims that the elite Jewish people run the Illuminati to propagate capitalism and communism, divide the world and eventually rule it.

There are still many other theorists who contemplate about secret societies, specifically the Illuminati and each theory is different from the other. For instance, Christian fundamentalists assert that the One World Government or in these modern times, the New World Order of the Illuminati is a sign of the arrival of the antichrist. This theory was supported by the American political advocacy group, John Birch Society, outlining the objective of secret societies such as the Illuminati.

In this chapter, some of the most talked-about events that are associated with Illuminati conspiracies will be discussed. In addition, a list of some celebrities who are allegedly Illuminati members as well as those supposedly silenced by the Order will be named.

Famous and (Alleged) Illuminati Conspiracies

The 9/11 Tragedy

One of the most aggressive and grievous events in the history of the United States of America is the 9/11 or the Twin Tower Tragedy. Most conspiracy theorists impute the tragedy to Illuminati's elaborate plan. The incident initiated the United States Government to engage in a war against global terrorism; thus, as the country needed funds to defeat its adversaries, it was exposed to the Illuminati. Conspiracy theorists claim that one of the styles common to secret societies is to send out predictions of their plans. Prior to the occurrence of the 9/11 tragedy, the cartoon series Johnny Bravo of Cartoon Network, aired an episode, which was very similar to the debacle.

Media Puppeteers

According to conspiracy theorists, most people have more knowledge about their favorite celebrities than their neighbors or co-workers. These theorists claim that this is all a part of the propaganda of the Illuminati, who controls and manipulates the media. The purpose of such control is to spread obsessive and ridiculous reports about celebrities to deviate the public's attention from more important matters such as the Government, revolutions, global politics, and rebellions. As the public loses track of these matters, the Illuminati are provided the opportunity to pull the strings of people.

<u>**Conspiracy Theories on Mysterious Assassinations and Deaths of Famous Personalities**</u>

Most conspiracy theorists also assert the association of the Order of the Illuminati to the mysterious deaths and assassinations of famous personalities not only in the United States but across the globe.

Abraham Lincoln

It was said that the Illuminati meant to assassinate Lincoln to stop him from aggressing huge businesses and corporations, which the latter considered as a threat not only to him but to the Southern Confederacy. The Illuminati planned the assassination to keep Lincoln from speaking against the Order. Lincoln was cited for his statement: *"The money powers prey upon the nation in times of peace and conspire against it in times of adversity. The banking powers are more despotic than a monarchy, more insolent than autocracy, more selfish than bureaucracy. They denounce as public enemies all who question their methods or throw light upon their crimes."* Consequently, Lincoln's assassination transpired on April 15, 1865.

John F. Kennedy

The 35th President of the United States was said to work with the Illuminati; however, when he started opposing to the objectives and practices of the Order, his assassination was mapped out. On November 22, 1963, JFK received two gunshots, one in the head, and one in the throat.

Lee Harvey Oswald

The sniper who assassinated JFK was said to be a victim of the Illuminati as well. During the assassination of JFK, Oswald was believed to be under the mind control of the Illuminati. However, Oswald was captured by the police. In order to keep Oswald from exposing the mastermind of JFK's assassination, he was shot while he was about to be transferred to a county jail on November 24, 1963, two days after JFK's assassination.

Martin Luther King, Jr.

Given that this man was very influential, he became a threat to the Illuminati. According to conspiracy theorists, MLK began to protest the Vietnam War, which at the time, provided significant financial benefits to many corporations. As such, the Illuminati planned a setting for MLK's assassination. The latter was shot on the balcony of a motel in Memphis on April 4, 1968.

John F. Kennedy, Jr.

Conspiracy theorists cannot help but compare the death of JFK Jr. to his father, JFK and believe that it was Illuminati's plan. Rumors regarding the knowledge of JFK, Jr. about his father's death spread across the United States. The rumors bore the involvement of George H. W. Bush and the CIA to the assassination of JFK. It was said that JFK, Jr. was prepared to publish the information he got when his plane crashed mysteriously. According to reports, the plane crashed due to pilot error. JFK, Jr. dreamed of becoming a pilot ever since he was a child; as such, he took flying lessons and got his flying license. JFK, Jr. died with his wife and sister-in-law.

John Lennon

Being a part of a famous group worldwide, John Lennon was viewed as a threat to many influential and powerful people. In fact, the Immigration and Naturalization Service (INS) made its attempts to deport Lennon. The Federal Bureau of Investigation (FBI) also placed him under surveillance. Apart from being a superstar, Lennon was also known as a political activist and a fighter for peace. He also recorded songs about anti-war. It is said that Lennon's assassin, Mark David Chapman, was associated with the Illuminati and that he was under their mind control when he shot Lennon on December 8, 1980.

Malcolm X

An American Muslim minister and a human rights activists, Malcolm X was considered a great threat to the Order of the Illuminati. He was referred to as the most influential African American who was opposed to the "power structure." On February 21, 1965, Malcolm X was shot with a sawed-off shotgun and semi-automatic handguns when he was about to speak to the Organization of the Afro-American in Manhattan.

Jim Morrison

Many conspiracy theorists believe that Morrison was a reptilian member of the Order of the Illuminati. He promoted "hippie counterculture rebellion" and generational gap through his music. In addition, his death is unconfirmed. Supposedly, on July 3, 1971, Morrison died of a heart attack; however, his death was not reported until three days later. Furthermore, many people attest that they have seen Morrison in scruffy areas across the globe since his supposed death. Most conspiracy theorists believe that the Illuminati faked Morrison's death.

Bruce Lee

Considered as the most influential martial artist ever to live, Lee was also known to change how Asians were presented in American movies. Prior to his death on July 20, 1973, Lee often told people surrounding him that he was being watched by a demon. He died of an allergic reaction to a painkiller. However, conspiracy theorists believe that Lee was an Illuminati sacrifice.

Grace Kelly

Most conspiracy theorists believe that the Illuminati arranged the marriage of Kelly to the Prince of Monaco, Rainier III. Kelly supposedly died in a car accident when she had a stroke. She was brought to the hospital; however, Rainier III asked the doctors to take off her life support on September 14, 1982, a day after the accident. It was believed that Kelly was no longer needed and she had to be sacrificed.

Kurt Cobain

Although he was very famous during his time, Cobain resented fame. He claimed that he only wanted to share his music. Conspiracy theorists assert that the Illuminati wanted to place Cobain under mind control; however, he refused. Thus, the Illuminati planned his death. Although his death was considered a suicide, many conspiracy theorists doubted the circumstances. Cobain died on April 5, 1994 from a gunshot wound.

Princess Diana

Many conspiracy theorists believe that the Royal family is very significant in the Order of the Illuminati. The separation of Prince Charles and Princess Diana was a huge embarrassment for the Royals. Although Princess Di was famous and well-loved not only in England but in most parts of the world, she was no longer a member of the Royal family. As such, she had to go. On August 31, 1997, Princess Di allegedly died of a car accident. However, the final verdict of the inquest on her death established that it was a murder rather than an accident.

Michael Jackson

Many people think that Jackson was a member of the Illuminati. However, prior to his death, he began speaking against the Order, saying that there was a conspiracy to defame him. Consequently, he was labeled as a "child-molester" and a "freak." La Toya Jackson, Michael's sister, claimed that his brother often spoke about a group of individuals trying to kill him. Just a few days prior to his comeback concert in London, Jackson died in his bed on June 25, 2009 due to acute intoxification of propofol and benzodiazepine, resulting in cardiac arrest. His personal physician was later convicted of involuntary manslaughter.

<u>Alleged Illuminati Celebrities</u>

One industry that bears the most influential and powerful people in the world is the showbiz industry. Given that the Order of the Illuminati is a collective of elite individuals, it is no wonder why they are inclined to penetrating the world of show business.

As mentioned in the previous chapters, the Illuminati make use of symbols that may not mean anything to ordinary people. However, to the members of the Order, the symbols are sacred and can also indicate whether or not a person is a member. Apart from the symbols mentioned earlier, others include goat heads, owls, and unicorns.

Illuminati members are not ordinary people. They are the world's elite including financial geniuses, politicians, and celebrities. The following is a list of alleged Illuminati celebrities who are considered the finest and most influential in their chosen fields.

Jay-Z

He is not just a rapper, but also considered the godfather of today's Illuminati. Those looking for proof can take note of how Jay-Z flashes the Pyramid symbol through hand gestures in his concerts and performances. He has also included goat heads in some of his music videos.

Beyoncé

Naturally, when the husband is the leader in propagating the views of the Illuminati, the wife comes in support. During the 2013 Super Bowl halftime show, Beyoncé flashed the Illuminati symbol Pyramid before millions of live, online, and home audiences. In addition, she also modelled a dress that featured a goat skull in a photo shoot. Jay-Z and Beyoncé's daughter, Blue Ivy, is believed to be the newest, if not, the youngest member of the Order, who may become another influential individual in the future.

Lindsay Lohan

It is being observed that Lohan flashes the triangle symbol each time she does a photoshoot or being photographed. Her tattoo is a devil red triangle with the statement "What Dreams May Come." Many believe that she is giving credit to the Illuminati for helping people achieve fame.

Lady Gaga

Just like Jay-Z and Beyoncé, Lady Gaga has also included goat heads in her music videos. She has also incorporated unicorns and triangle icons to her album covers and videos, which indicates the "immaculate conception" of the Illuminati. Lady Gaga allegedly admitted of having a dream that involved Lindsay Lohan, riding a goat towards the mountain of pyramids to meet the Lizard Queen, no other than Lady Gaga. Consequently, this dream prompted her to perform an Illuminati ritual in various shows.

Rihanna

Given that Jay-Z is her mentor and she is his protégé, it is no wonder that Rihanna is also a member of the Illuminati. In fact, she does not hesitate revealing it in her concerts. Rihanna is often observed showing off the Pyramid symbol using hand gestures. She even flashed a headline that she is the "Princess of the Illuminati" in her "S&M" video. Riri was also rumored to be the "Rihanna" in a story that involved a secret Mexican goat farm.

Madonna

During her 2012 Super Bowl halftime performance, Madonna included a human pyramid and wore horns on her helmet. It should also be interesting to note that two alleged members of the Illuminati, Beyoncé and Madonna, top-billed the halftime show two years on the run. It may be a coincidence; however, it can also be possible that the NFL is also affiliated with the Illuminati.

Kanye West

It is a fact that Jay-Z and Kanye West are good friends and that they are likewise professionally close to each other. Thus, it is highly possible that Kanye is also a member of the Illuminati. Kanye always wears jewelry that features symbols of the Order. He also includes occult imagery in his music videos.

Celine Dion

Rumor has it that Celine's music is the work of the devil. This is after flashing Illuminati symbols for throwing up the "El Diablo" or Devil's Horns gesture in her performances and shows. Although she is not as visible as Jay-Z, Beyoncé, Lady Gaga, Rihanna, and other music artists, she is known to "recruit" or fraternize other bigwigs in the showbiz industry. Some assert that her eyes are literally shaped as the number 6, a number that Illuminati members are fond of.

Justin Bieber

Ever since he wore shirts with pentagrams and flashing the "A-Ok" symbol, Bieber is now being accused as being part of the Order of the Illuminati. Although many people may think that he might be just "A-Ok," some contest that there is something behind those pentagram-designed shirts and his flashing "A-Ok." He also loves goat farms just as Rihanna does.

Emma Watson

She was photographed framing her eye with the number 6. That piece of evidence sparked the issue that she may be an Illuminati member. Many could not fathom how gorgeous she looks; how she has such fabulous hair; how she finished her college education in spite of her busy schedules; and how she pulled through with her speech on feminism at the United Nations. These people think that it's all the work of the Illuminati.

Angelina Jolie

Her choices in movie roles, outrageous personal life, and wearing of a vial of Brad Pitt's blood are all very Illuminati. These are the reasons that many people believe that Jolie is a part of the shadow group. Apart from these, she has also posed with a satanic hand gesture. A number of her movies, specifically the Tomb Raider series involved motifs of the "all-seeing eye" symbol.

Paris Hilton

From an early age, it is said that Hilton was educated in the ways of the Order of the Illuminati. Her family is excessively wealthy. Her music videos also include symbols of the Order. She also flashes the "Shh" hand gesture not only in her photos but guest appearances as well. Many people believe it is a gesture that pays tribute to the Illuminati, if not, she may be brainwashed by the secret society.

Chris Brown

Although he is the ex-boyfriend of another alleged Illuminati member, Rihanna, Brown has exposed himself as a member of the secret society through his choice of tattoos. One of them is a snake that has a red pyramid with an eye at the tip of its tail. He almost always performs half-naked or in tank tops to give credit to the Illuminati through his tattoo on his back.

Dr. Dre

His best-selling "Beats by Dre" headphones and his affiliations with some celebrities included in this list make people believe that he is a member of the Illuminati. His headphones are featured in many music videos of the other alleged Illuminati celebrities. In fact, these celebrities have also promoted Dre's headphones rather excessively. The anagram for "Beats" is "Beast," which suggests his affiliation with the shadow group.

Sean Combs

His wealth and influence in the music industry are just some indicators of his affiliation with the Illuminati. However, he further confirmed his membership to the shadow group through flashing satanic hand gestures and the Pyramid symbol. Given that he is extremely influential, his presence will be of great benefit to the Illuminati when the New World Order is set in place.

Conclusion

Thank you again for downloading this book!

I hope this book was able to help you learn more about the Illuminati!

The Order of the Illuminati's story is revealed or repressed, exposed, exaggerated, or ridiculed many times depending on the point of view of authors and critics. Obtaining the absolute truth about the Illuminati can be very challenging given that the group is "secret" in nature. Various versions of the story of the Illuminati have emerged through the years. Some may be facts while others are pure fabrications. As mentioned, it all depends on the author and critics as well as the audience they cater to.

While it is not possible to resolve all questions about the Illuminati, this book merely tried to draw a clearer picture of the Order, its goals and objectives, the nature of its members, and the present facts that are associated with the secret society.

Much of the information presented is simply the theories of various people. It is up to you to decide what to believe, and who you think may be a part of this infamous organization.

Finally, if you enjoyed this book, please take the time to share your thoughts and post a review on Amazon. It'd be greatly appreciated!

Thank you and good luck!